© TRUE TALES of RESCUE ©

Anteater Adventure

KAMA EINHORN

PHOTOGRAPHS BY ELLA BARON

HOUGHTON MIFFLIN HARCOURT
Boston   New York

The text type was set in Jolly Good Sans.

Library of Congress Cataloging-in-Publication Data
Names: Einhorn, Kama, 1969- author.
Title: Anteater adventure / Kama Einhorn.
Description: Boston : Houghton Mifflin Harcourt, [2019] |
Series: True talesof rescue ; 4 | Audience: Age 7-10. | Audience: Grade 4 to 6. |
Includesbibliographical references and index.
Identifiers: LCCN 2018034239 | ISBN 9781328767042 (hardcover)
Subjects: LCSH: Myrmecophagidae--Anecdotes--Juvenile literature. |
Wildliferescue--Anecdotes--Juvenile literature.
Classification: LCC QL737.E24 E36 2019 | DDC 599.3/14--dc23
LC record available at https://lccn.loc.gov/2018034239

Manufactured in Malaysia
TWP 10 9 8 7 6 5 4 3 2 1
4500747136

This book is inspired by the true stories of the Tamandua Refuge, and it is full of real facts about anteaters and sanctuary life. But it's also "creative" nonfiction—because anteaters don't talk, at least not in ways that humans can understand! Some anteaters mentioned are combinations of several different ones, and certain details—including locations, events, and timing—have been changed, and some human dialogue has been reconstructed from memory.

This book is not a manual on how to rescue wildlife, or provide any actual directions on caring for anteaters or any other species. Every situation and every animal is different. If you see an animal in trouble, contact a licensed wildlife rehabilitator right away.

For Ella Baron

And for Ian Anderson
and the whole Caves Branch team

CONTENTS

HOPE & HAVEN:
ANIMAL SANCTUARIES

A sanctuary is a safe place where living beings are kept safe from harm and are free to be themselves.

Humans have created *animal* sanctuaries—protected places for injured, orphaned, or threatened animals. In a sanctuary, animals prepare to return to the wild. If that's not an option, the animals spend the rest of their lives there, in as natural a habitat as possible.

Anteaters, who live in the rainforest, do have natural predators—snakes, birds of prey, margays, and jaguars—but most animal sanctuaries exist because of harm done by people. Humans have cut down trees to build houses or buildings, forcing anteaters (known as tamandua in Belize) and other wildlife out of their treetop homes. Humans have put roads through animals' territories, making wildlife more likely to be hit by cars. Anteaters may be attacked by unleashed dogs. Some people consider anteaters to be weird or scary, and they mistreat them; hunters trap them

At sanctuaries, humans lend a helping hand.

to keep them or sell them illegally as pets. Extreme weather (such as hurricanes and floods) also harms anteaters.

The people who run sanctuaries are serious about their work, but they all wish they didn't have to do it in the first place. They wish that there was no more need for these places, and that the world was safer for animals.

There is plenty of heartbreak in any sanctuary's story, but there's also lots of happy news. Most sanctuary owners teach people about local wildlife

and how to protect animals and share the land with them. The more you know about why sanctuaries are important and what people can do to help, the better off all animals—in your neighborhood and all over the planet—will be.

SANCTUARY STEPS

Each sanctuary is different, but they all do some or all of the following things, in the order below. Tamandua Refuge handles all four phases:

- **Rescue:** Humans step in, remove animals from harm, and bring them to safety. Rescue situations are usually emergencies.

- **Recovery:** Licensed wildlife caregivers treat the animals for injuries or illnesses, create a recovery plan, and let them rest and heal.

- **Rehabilitation:** The caregivers encourage the animals' natural instincts. Some things have to be taught; some the animals know instinctively. Sometimes, animals learn from one another.

- **Release:** Using a careful (sometimes very slow!) process, caregivers help animals return to their natural habitats whenever possible.

PART 1

RESCUE

Helping Hands

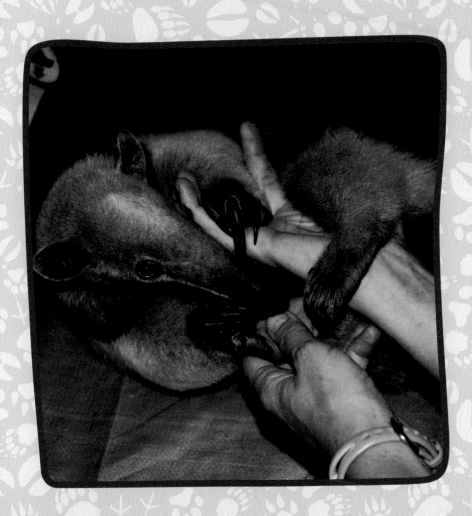

CHAPTER 1

A NEW DAY

I slept through the whole hurricane last night. I'm just opening my tiny eyes now as Ella, the human who's been caring for me, opens the veranda door and the thick, humid jungle air moves slowly through my pen.

I lift my head from the termite nest I've been using as a pillow, point my long snout high, and sniff. Something's gone horribly wrong out there. The smells swirling around me are all messed up.

I know this better than most creatures in the rainforest, even if I've been stuck inside for a few months with my broken leg. It smells as if nature put the whole rainforest into a blender and then poured it out.

My heartbeat is even stronger than usual.
It's more like a heart-*boom!* Ella always tells
people that when she puts her hand on my
chest, it feels like someone's thumping and
banging on it from the inside—hard,
like a drum.

Good morning. I'm Abi.

11

The ceiling's dripping in a few places near my pen in the living room, and Ella's frantically using towels and a few plastic containers to clean up all the water as fast as she can. She quietly checks over my pen to make sure water isn't dripping on my head.

Like all anteaters, I hate rain and wind. In the wild, it's no problem, because I'd be covered by the canopy—the thick roof of the rainforest. The canopy is like an umbrella, but it's twenty feet (6 meters) thick and up to eighty feet (24 meters) off the ground (as high as a ten-story building!). It's dark, warm, and moist. The rainforest is a very drippy place. If things hadn't gone wrong recently, I'd be spending most of my time up there, unless I was on the rainforest floor sniffing around for fallen fruit, insects, or grubs.

Now I hear trees cracking and falling, branches snapping, and chainsaws running. People are cutting fallen trees into pieces, then carting them down to the river in wheelbarrows so that everyone will be able to safely walk around and drive in and out of this place, which is called Caves Branch Lodge.

Ella Baron and her husband, Ian Anderson, run the lodge, where guests sleep in jungle bungalows or treehouses and learn about the rainforest (the tourists don't come near me, as I'm not supposed to be around humans). Their home is right there on the same property, and I live in their living room. Plenty of people work to run the lodge, but they don't usually come into the house.

Right now, Ella is sweaty and upset. She's bringing in dog and cat carriers, but they're not full of cats and dogs. They're full of birds

that were injured in the storm. I can smell them. The front door is constantly opening and closing. There are too many humans coming in and out, and all the different smells are exhausting me. It's a lot of information to take in. Everyone's trying to help the birds, trying to get their walkie-talkies set up, and trying to get the Wi-Fi and phones working so they can all have contact with the outside world.

Ella needs to call or e-mail her staff to see if they're okay and, if they are, to ask them to come and help. And she has to let everyone know that she and Ian are okay, even though much of their land and property has been damaged. A lot of the canopy has come down. Ella has to call the bird rescue people for advice about all those poor birds, many of them babies thrown from their nests onto the rainforest floor.

Oh dear, now she's bringing in a boa constrictor (in a plastic carrier, of course!). The snake was in the floodwaters, and Ella didn't want him or her to get hacked by a scared employee with a machete—that's a big knife—as everyone uses machetes around here to clear paths through the jungle. She'll release him once the waters have gone down. There's also an opossum and her eleven babies in a crate on the porch. No one here is having a very good morning.

"I knew it was going to be bad," Ella says to Marvin Paredes, whom works in the botanical gardens. He's come into the house to get a walkie-talkie. "The soldier ants were so busy in the citrus groves yesterday," she adds. "They knew it was their last chance to eat for a while."

From my pen, I can see the kitchen, the couch, the office area, and the entrance, and it's all a mess. Ella's muddy machete is lying on the coffee table. There are also two tubs of termite nests that she gathered for me yesterday, but she and I both know that they're already a bit stale—and that there will be no more for a few days, until the roads clear. It's not a great situation, but she always makes sure I eat something, even if she has to open the mealworm container in the freezer. And there's always plenty of fermented fruit in the kitchen ... *Mmm.* To humans it looks rotten, but it's not.

This place is usually much more organized than it seems at the moment. Ella's helped fifteen of us anteaters here (I'm number fifteen!) over the years. It's Ella and Ian's home, but Ella calls our pens the Tamandua

Refuge. All but one of the anteaters before me have made it back to the wild.

Some of us stay a whole year, but I've been here only a few months. We usually stay away from other mammals (anteaters included; a group of anteaters is called a parade, but you'd never see us in a group), but I had to make an exception for Ella because I wanted to live and get back to the rainforest. And I'm so ready to go. But clearly I'm going be stuck here a little longer, at least until the floodwaters go down. So I've got some time to tell you stuff.

I'm really lucky I was inside last night. Like most wildlife, we anteaters do very badly in hurricanes and other bad weather. In fact, it was just after a flash flood ten years ago that Ella rescued her first anteater, Gabi,

from the river's muddy floodwaters. Gabi was only eight weeks old, and she'd gotten separated from her mom. Just like today, lots of wildlife had been hurt or killed during that flood.

Gabi and I never met, or course. But I can't tell you my story without telling you hers, because Ella learned everything she knows about rescuing anteaters from Gabi. Plus, my name, Abi, is an echo of Gabi's name! (It's

When Ella rescued me, I was so thirsty.
I had no choice but to trust her.

My whole body is screaming up, up, up!
These cohune trees grow all over my real home.

just a coincidence—I was named after Abe,
the man who found me and called for help.)

Ella talks about Gabi (and all the other
anteaters Ella rescued) all the time. She
teaches vet students, and she visits schools
all around Belize. And she's always talking
about us to Ian and her botanical garden

staff, teaching them, asking for their help.

If Ella had never rescued Gabi, I probably wouldn't even be alive right now.

But my story is very different from Gabi's. For one thing, I wasn't a baby when I was rescued. Still, certain things are always the same with us anteaters, especially when we're in trouble. Ella observes us, figures out how to take good care of us, and gives us the best chance of going back to live in the canopy of the rainforest. That's where Gabi is now.

I hear Ella tell Ian that she didn't think Gabi's area was damaged too badly by this storm.

I sure hope that's true. Gabi and Ella certainly worked hard to get her back out there.

Gabi and Ella. I've lived with Ella for a while now. Gabi and I have never met, of course, but I feel as if I really know her.

CHAPTER 2

ANTEATER ACADEMY

Ella comes back from checking on the generator that will keep the electricity going, and she lugs up huge bottles of drinking water from the emergency storage shed down the hill. Looks like they'll be eating lots of peanut butter, crackers, and coffee over the next few days.

The Wi-Fi is mostly out, and it's driving the people berserk. Oh man, there's *nothing* like a human without Wi-Fi.

No matter. Ella still brings me breakfast: half an avocado and more of yesterday's termites. She also offers me half of a seedy bright-magenta dragon fruit. But I'm not in the mood for dragon fruit, and I swat it away—*really hard!*—with my claw. Ella chuckles and seems impressed. Gabi used to do this too. Then I use

my claws and nose to mash up the avocado a little, and just like Gabi, I get it all over my snout. I make my usual lip-smacking, snuffling sounds.

Then I stick my head into a blue plastic bin and flick my long, sticky tongue deep in to pull up the tiny, tasty treasures—hundreds of termites from their nest! The nest looks like a hard, rocky sponge, but it's actually made of termite spit and poop.

Anyway, while poor Ella and her team keep working, I'll tell you the facts. I'm a northern tamandua, to be specific.

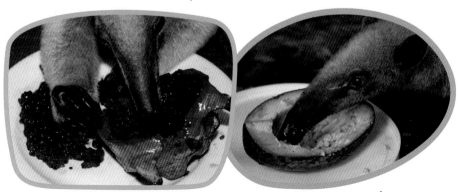

Dragon fruit for dinner!

I adore avocados.

23

EVERYTHING I NEED

Everything I need at the moment is right here:

🐾 **Branches:** Ella and her team built us a "tree" by tying some branches together and screwing some right into the wall. There are also thick, dry, ropy vines.

- 🐾 **Logs:** Three dry orange trees are stacked together for me to climb on.

- 🐾 **Jungle Bin:** This tub smells like home. It's filled with things from our real habitat: a variety of wood, flowers, and leaves.

- 🐾 **Termite Tub:** Ella stores termite nests in big plastic bins.

- 🐾 **The Dog Crate:** I lived in this when I first got here, but now I just use it as a hiding place.

- 🐾 **Hiding Boxes:** Ella built little wooden boxes in the branches for when we want to hide up high.

- 🐾 **My Toilet:** There's a container of water in the corner for me to poop in. In the wild, we climb up and poop from up high into a creek or river. And there is a towel in the one corner where I always go to pee.

- 🐾 **A Thick Fleece Blanket:** This is mostly for pups who can't keep themselves warm, but it's nice to have if I'm chilly.

- 🐾 **Hammocks:** Little cloth beds made of T-shirts for extra climbing help and resting.

In Spanish, I'm called *oso hormiguero* (ant-eating bear)! *Tamandua* comes from two Tupi Indian words: *taa* (ant) and *mandeu* (trap). We're related to sloths and armadillos. We tamanduas eat mostly termites, which make the name *anteater* kind of confusing. But we like ants, too!

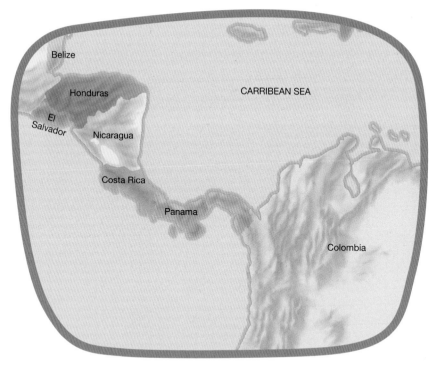

Anteaters live in Central and South America.

26

Ella is a botanist (a plant scientist) specializing in epiphytes (plants that live on other plants). Epiphytes hold water, and animals can drink from them as if they're little cups! Ella runs the botanical garden here at Caves Branch. She knows things about rainforest plants and animals that most people don't know. She loves looking at flowers, plants, bugs . . . and us.

Ella gives tours and lectures about rainforest ecology. Scientists come from all over the world to meet Ella and see Caves Branch. The botanical garden is a marvel, with the largest orchid collection in Belize. There's an orchid here that's as tiny as a grain of rice!

Speaking of marvels . . . let me tell you about our amazing bodies, using Gabi as a model.

Here's Gabi! We weigh up to 11 pounds (about the size of cats).

Our markings look like vests!

Our tails wrap and grip, like a monkey's. We use them as "third legs" to balance as we stand.

Just like fingerprints, each tail pattern is unique.

Our strong stomachs grind insects, as teeth would.

28

Our twisty ribcages let us eat in any position.

Our faces are fuzzy. Our wiry fur helps protect us from insect bites.

Our ears let us hear termites chewing in a tree trunk.

We don't see well. A third eyelid shields our eyeballs from pesky insects.

We can smell 40 times better than humans. Our noses know!

Our claws are shiny weapon—glossy and sharp. We walk on our "knuckles" to protect our palm pads.

Our mouths only open a tiny crack. We're toothless!

Our foot-long tongues dart and flick into nests 200 times a minute. They're attached right to our stomachs.

And Here's Ella

1. Ella's **eyes** are always watching, observing, seeing details, noticing what others don't notice. She remembers paths through the jungle, paths others don't take.

2. Her **ears** help her identify the smallest differences in our sounds: snuffle, snort, hiss, and grunt (we fart, too)! She can identify many different birdsongs, and knows how high the river is just by listening. At night, she enjoys the orchestra of giant frogs, cicadas, howler monkeys, and toucans—the musicians in our rainforest symphony.

3. If Ella's awake, her **hands** are busy. They may be holding a notebook and pencil, tapping a keyboard, mashing our food, holding us, using a machete, or working in the gardens. She wears a big leather glove wrapped in duct tape for extra protection.

4. Her **arms and legs** are strong from tough garden work and just living in the rainforest. She has good balance (not as good as ours, though!), which helps her on muddy, rocky walks.

5. Insects constantly bite her **skin**, and she can't even put on bug repellent or use any lotion or ointment on the bites, because the smell freaks us out!

6. Ella's **brain** never stops learning. She spends a lot of time researching ... and watching us. We seem mysterious to most humans—we live up high and move around at night. But sometimes Ella tries to forget that she's human, so she can experience the world as an anteater. When she's caring for us, her brain starts working differently.

CHAPTER 3
TAMANDUA MAMA

Ten years ago, on a terrible day a lot like today, Gabi arrived. There had been a flash flood. The river was high, muddy, and loud.

A guest ran up to Ian in the group dining room, where everyone was taking a break from clearing the damage from the muddy water. Empty coffee mugs, water bottles, and granola bars were everywhere. Sticky clay mud, muddy water, leaves, and broken branches covered everything.

The guest was freaked out. "Ian!" he cried. "There's a strange animal flopping around and screaming on the riverbank!" They went to look. The animal was so dirty and wet that Ian could barely tell it was an anteater. He picked up the trembling thing with a towel

Gabi was as tiny as a kitten.

and set her down gently in a dry cardboard
box, then tucked in some more towels. She
had wounds on her head and abdomen.
From the lodge office, Ian called the Belize
Zoo and the forestry department, who said
that since the roads were flooded and they
didn't know anyone else who rehabilitated
anteaters, they would give him a permit
to help this little creature until it could be
released into the wild.

33

When Ian entered the house, Ella sighed and gave him a horrible look. "Just leave that box on the porch, please! I've seen too many dead birds today, Ian. And I couldn't help most of them—all the roads to the bird rescue centers are flooded."

"Oh, this is no bird, my love," Ian said. "Come see." Like all the others who would come after her, the baby anteater was very scared. Gabi pressed herself into the corner of the box and tried to disappear. (Our faces don't show our feelings, but our bodies sure do!)

Ella peeked in at the shivering thing. "Is it a rat?" she asked a little nervously. "Do you think I can touch it? Or does it bite?"

"It's a baby anteater," Ian said. "I've never seen an anteater so close. Don't worry—they don't have teeth!"

Ella picked up the towel with the pup inside,
but she felt no warmth coming from its wet
little body. "Poor little boo-boo," she said.
"She's cold. Her mom must have gotten
washed away by the river."

"Sounds about right," Ian said, and added,
"I've gotta get back down to the crew. I'll be
home as soon as I can. This work's gonna
be endless."

Ella dried the pup off with another towel,
but it still felt cold. She'd heard that when
human babies are born, especially if
they're born too early, it's important to
have skin-to-skin contact for warmth. So
she held the anteater against her bare
skin under her T-shirt. The pup warmed
up right away and started clinging to Ella's
arms with her sharp claws. She didn't
seem afraid.

When Ella's teenage son, Gabe, came home, Ella put her finger to her lips and motioned for him to come close to show him what she had.

"Wow," Gabe said, staring. "You should name her Gabi, Mom, so you can pretend you're talking to me when you miss me once I go back to school in the fall." He smiled.

From then on, the strange little creature was Gabi, and Ella was "tamandua mama."

Ella had friends who rescued wildlife, so she knew it was all about keeping things dark, warm, and quiet for babies—dark like the rainforest canopy, warm like their moms, and quiet as in no human sounds. In a dark, quiet room, Gabi relaxed and stayed against Ella's warm skin for forty-eight hours straight as Ella used a syringe to put little drops of water and fruit juice into her mouth. Finally

Gabi opened her eyes and looked right at Ella. That's where this whole story really begins.

While holding Gabi close, Ella researched anteater care online and contacted zoos all over Central and South America for information. Ella figured out that Gabi was about two months old (though she weighed less than she should have), so she would still have been nursing. She was too young to eat termites, and no one seemed to have a recipe for anteater mom's milk. But once Ella talked to a number of anteater experts, she had a list of different suggestions. She told herself that since she was a scientist, she'd experiment until she figured it out. She started with goat milk and dry puppy food that she ground to powder in a blender.

The road to the vet was still flooded, and even though it seemed like a kooky idea,

Ella asked her family's doctor—a "people doctor"—to examine Gabi, and he said to bring her in. "I guess a mammal's a mammal," Ella thought, grateful for any help at all. The doctor basically treated Gabi as if she were a human baby. He listened to her heartbeat and lungs and weighed her. Then he cleaned and disinfected her wounds, checked for broken bones, and took a pee sample.

Ella's goal was to get the pup back to the wild, not keep it as a pet. That meant playing by anteater rules and being an anteater mom. Ella quieted her human mind and started thinking as the helpless animal would, trying to connect what she was reading with what she was observing.

At home, as soon as Ella was able to remove Gabi from her chest, Gabi began to explore

the veranda a little, still staying close to Ella's feet. In about two minutes, Gabi had biting ants crawling on her fur. She started climbing up Ella's leg very fast. Ella was in shock, and her skin was quickly covered in bright red scratches from Gabi's sharp claws.

Gabi would get irritated if Ella ever moved too far away from her. She'd make a little screaming noise and then be a little rough, climbing back onto Ella!

39

When Gabi reached Ella's shoulders, Ella
covered her face to protect her eyes
and tried to make some sense out of the
situation. Then Gabi wrapped her tail around
her "mom's" neck and started pressing her
body against Ella's head, grabbing tightly to
Ella's short hair.

Gabi had clearly reached her destination.
Ella's skin burned from the scratches, and
her own heart thumped loudly. She could
feel the ants move away from Gabi's body to
her own shoulders. *Ack!* Gabi had found her
comfort zone; Ella's head, neck, and back
were the closest things she could find to her
mom's back. About two seconds later, Gabi
was snoozing.

With four pounds of anteater on her head,
Ella knew there was no turning back. Over

the next few weeks, Ian and Gabe helped out
by preparing Gabi's foods and juices and
holding Gabi for short periods of time so
that Ella could take a shower and stretch her
aching neck. Sometimes when Gabe was doing
his homework, Ella would move Gabi onto his
head, but Gabi refused to spend more than a
half hour away from Ella's head. (I didn't spend
any time on Ella's head. I was four months old
when I was rescued . . . a little older than Gabi
had been, and much bigger.)

So Ella continued her life and work as much
as she could. It was quite a sight for guests
to see—a woman digging and planting in the
botanical gardens with an "anteater hat"!
At least Gabi slept through the night. (Even
though tamanduas are nocturnal, they follow
their moms' ways, so she adapted to Ella's
schedule.)

Ella found some termite nests in the botanical gardens, and she walked Gabi there every day. Ella would kneel down to the ground, and Gabi would scurry down to eat, never out of Ella's sight. Soon enough, Gabi had memorized the locations of the nests, plus areas with nonbiting ants.

Ella's skin was covered in bug bites, as Gabi couldn't be around bug spray. Ella just tried to relax and accept bites, scratches, and constant physical contact as part of life as an anteater mom. But there would be a lot more to accept.

Gabi couldn't be around other humans—

it wouldn't be good for her chances of release into the wild one day. So Ella's social life ended quickly, except for a few times when she, Ian, and Gabe visited their friends' place. Ella stood thirty feet away from everyone, with Gabi on her head. The friends had found some good termite nests on their land, and Ella took Gabi to the nests. The friends brought Ella a plate of food to eat while she supervised Gabi there, as the other humans ate at a table indoors. Ella and Gabi always stayed outside as long as it took for Gabi to eat all the termites in the nest.

Ella knew that her behavior may have seemed odd to others. Noise and fast movements would stress Gabi out, so Ella had to be silent all the time and move very slowly. Gabe gave Ella some science fiction audiobooks, which she found hilarious: she had a "real" alien in her life . . . wrapped around her head,

actually. In the stories, the space crews were trying to learn about alien cultures on other planets, and here was Ella, on Earth, trying to understand this unfamiliar creature.

It reminded her of the time when Gabe was a baby. She'd had to constantly watch him, making sure he didn't hurt himself, but at the same time she had to help him as he learned to crawl and walk. Of course, this new baby

Things got weird.

was learning to climb trees and find her own insects. But just as she had with Gabe, Ella learned what to do by trial and error, making mistakes until she got it right.

Life continued like this until Gabi was big, strong, and confident.

By the time I arrived here, ten years later, it was as if Ella had both created and graduated from Anteater Academy. Gabi and the others had been good professors. Ella learned to be a teacher herself—to the anteaters who needed to learn to be wild. She also started making presentations to vet students and schoolkids all over Belize.

Okay, now it's my turn to tell you about how I got here!

The problem is, there's a lot I don't remember.

Ella doesn't know more than I do, just this: I was old enough to be away from my mom sometimes. I spent most of my time in the canopy, but all of a sudden I was on the ground, and I didn't know what had happened. Some teenage boys saw that I was in trouble. They ran for their dad, Abe, who picked me up and put me a few feet off the ground in a fig tree, hoping I'd climb up farther on my own.

But I couldn't. I just sat there all night long, not moving. My left front leg and my right eye were both hurting me. When Abe checked the tree in the morning, he wrapped me in a towel and set me into a wooden crate that he found in his toolshed. I was scared, but I didn't fight him. He looked right into my eyes, and I felt shy. I just curled up in the box on my side, as my leg was most comfortable that way.

Ella can only guess how I got hurt. Strong

wind or rain may have knocked me off the branch in the canopy. Maybe I fell, maybe a branch poked my eye. And she doesn't know why I wasn't with my mom in the first place. My mom may have been taken by a human to be sold as a pet. She may have been hit by a car, hurt on an electric wire, or attacked by a predator. Or, just like Gabi, I could have been carried away by a rough river. Whatever happened, it wasn't good.

Anyway, Abe was a kind man. "We're gonna get you help, little buddy. . . . I just have to figure out how," he said. Just as Ella had done for Gabi long ago, he went online. He found the Belize Wildlife Clinic (which hadn't existed ten years earlier).

The clinic vet called her local anteater expert—Ella, of course! Ella drove her truck to meet Abe and me. She thanked Abe for

helping me, carefully took the box, and took me straight to the clinic, where I got a full exam. The vet was worried that I had parasites, worms, larva, or mites on me, but I didn't. She put some ointment in my eye. My leg felt awful, but I wasn't moving enough for Ella or the vet to be sure what the problem was. They knew they couldn't just plop me back into a tree, so they decided that Ella would take me home, observe me closely, and stay in touch with the vet.

Here at the refuge, Ella let me settle down alone in the dark for a while, then started quietly talking to me and offering termites and water. She touched me gently, trying to find the spots I'd allow her to touch. Gabi must have taught Ella all of this. It was easy for me to trust her.

I used her palm to steady myself as I ate my

first indoor termites. (Later, I'd sit on her arm as I ate them!) I drank water, and Ella put more ointment on my eye. But as she watched me move a little, she soon saw that I couldn't use my front leg.

Sigh. An X-ray showed that my leg was broken, and I needed surgery. The vet put a pin in my bone so it could grow back together. Ella stayed with me the whole time.

The X-ray confirmed Ella's hunch.

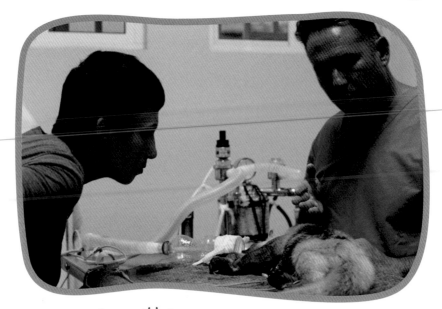

Ella watched everything.
She wanted to learn
as much as she could
about my insides.

The vet's team
made sure that my
pulse stayed normal
during the operation.

Back home, Ella became my nurse and my physical therapist. I was all stitched up, and very uncomfortable. Ella had to change the bandages covering my scars. She snuck my medicine and vitamins into my coconut water.

Ella was supposed to keep me still—no climbing or running—for *eight weeks*, to let my bone heal! She had dealt with lots of challenging situations with us tamanduas, but now she had the unfortunate job of stopping me from climbing. That was a shame, because it's what I was born to do.

Plus, unlike Gabi, *I* stayed up all night. At midnight I'd scratch the metal door of the carrier, and Ella would wake up and let me out. My routine was the same every night: come out slowly, sniff around to check that

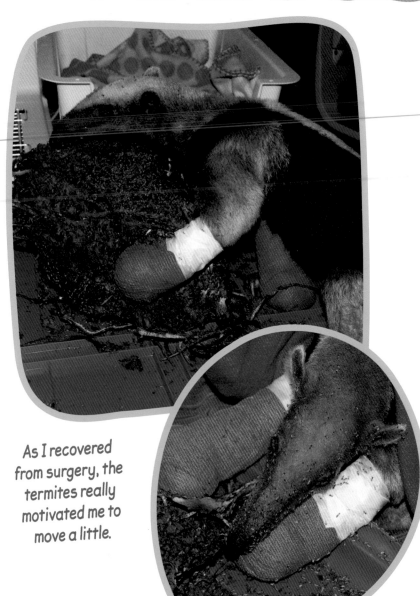

As I recovered from surgery, the termites really motivated me to move a little.

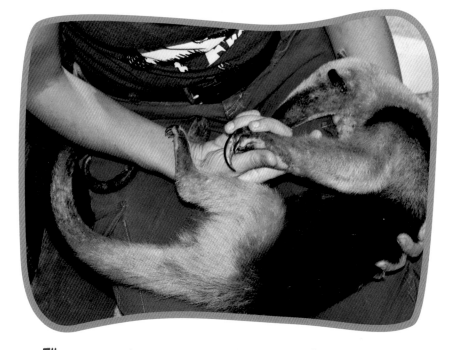

*Ella massaged me three times a day to help my muscles heal.
She even tried acupressure.*

everything is exactly the same, drink from
my water bowl for a long time, and pee on my
towel in the corner.

Then Ella would take me to the Plexiglas pen. It
had smooth plastic walls that made it (almost!)
impossible for me to climb. To distract me from

trying to climb, Ella had different kinds of ferns, rotten logs, bromeliads, and orchids on the floor. She thought I'd be safe alone in this pen. Ha! It took me a few days, but I was finally successful in making a little hole to hold onto. Next thing Ella knew I'm outta there, using my three good legs to climb up and over the wall. Ella put an end to this adventure and returned to her job of being next to me all night long. Oh well.

I got Ella to play my games—wrapping myself around her arm and then clawing very gently at her fingers. I felt kind of sorry for her that she didn't have wonderful claws like mine. I'd try to bend her fingers, and sometimes I'd press my claws a little hard into her skin, though I was still very gentle.

Eight long weeks later, I was allowed to run, and I ran around in circles. I had a new X-ray taken, and it showed that my leg bone had healed, so

I had *another* surgery to take the pin out. On the way to the surgery, I was so unhappy in the small plastic carrier that I hacked a tiny hole in its "ceiling" with my big claw. Then I kept hacking, hacking, hacking until the tip of

Ella always knew exactly what I needed.

my claw could poke through to the outside. When we got to the vet, he and Ella had a good laugh. "Looks like someone's getting wild," the vet said, smiling.

Recovering from that surgery was easier, and I graduated to the small pen. I could finally start climbing a bit. A week later, I graduated to the big pen. Ella still had to check on me, feed me, give me my vitamins, and clean up after me, but I already knew what I needed to know in order to go back to my habitat. Ella's job got easier—now she just had to leave me alone and observe me, making sure I continued in the right direction.

PART 2

RECOVERY

Creature Care

CHAPTER 4

HOTEL TAMANDUA

Ella doesn't use human words with us tamanduas very much, but we definitely have conversations with her. Our communication feels something like this:

> **Ella:** *Don't worry. I'll take care of everything. I'll do anything to make sure you get back home. Oh, I really hope you understand me.*

> **Us:** *I appreciate it. I need termites.*

> **Ella:** *Of course.*

> **Us:** *I trust you completely.*

> **Ella:** *I'm so happy you do. I got this.*

Ella's a bit like the owner of a hotel. Just as in a regular hotel, where the staff tries to take care

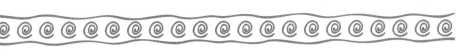

of everything, Ella cleans my pen while I sleep, and she thinks of every tiny thing I may need.

She's always busy, but she always makes time to write observations in her field journal.

Friday, midnight

It's not bedtime until Gabi's belly is full of termites, and that can take hours. It's like having a newborn all over again. But I keep watching, learning, following her lead, and letting her teach me what to do next. I just have to slow down and patiently observe, the same as I do on my field expeditions to find rare plants.

What else can I do? I can't exactly argue with her. Her instincts are telling her what she needs to do, and my job is to help her do it. I just try to interpret her demands and provide what she needs from moment to moment. That's the only way to keep her calm and happy, and to help her heal and grow.

Gabi liked to be warm, and her feet got cold easily. Ella had been right; Gabi had needed Ella's body to keep warm. When sleeping with Ella, she relaxed. And like me, she liked massages.

Since being "home" means feeling safe and comfortable, we pups get stuffed anteaters to hold on to anytime we want. We have our choice of sizes! But starting when Gabi was about four months old, the only way she'd fall asleep was by holding Ella's thumb and squeezing it very gently for about half an hour.

Of course, we're not here because we were dying to have a human mom. We're here because we don't have our own moms anymore, and for now we can't live in our real homes. But like any mom, Ella makes sure we have safe places to stay.

We like to squeeze our stuffed anteaters with our claws, just the way we'd hang tight to our moms. I used to grab onto two at once!

So here are our accommodation options once we are rescued.

Homes Away from Home

HOTEL TAMANDUA

The emergency transport crate is always good for a belly-up snooze.

↶ CAT CARRIER:

We usually arrive in a container (or even a wood crate or cardboard box), but we don't stay there very long. It's just for emergency transport.

It would have been dangerous for me to really climb, but I still needed to nestle in branches, so this was perfect.

↶ LARGE DOG CARRIER:

Ella screwed branches inside this carrier. Gabi and I both stayed in the large dog carrier for a few weeks after our rescues.

☙ THE LITTLE PEN:

Once it's safe for us to climb a little, we go to a little pen in the living room. The branches here are low, and the floor is soft in case we fall (there's a foam mat under a tarp or a plastic liner). If we're babies and have never learned to climb in the first place, the branches will help inspire us. They're strong, so they don't bend and sway and knock us off balance. There's wire on top so we can't climb out.

In the little pen, we can climb from hammock to hammock and rest safely.

Dozing in my favorite hammock!

I'm in the big pen now.

The fences in the jungle house are covered with palm fronds so we can't see out. Knowing we're
trapped can make us a little nuts, so at first Ella took Gabi there for an hour at a time.

℅ **THE BIG PEN:** This is the same as the little pen, just larger and with higher branches, plus ropes and straps for climbing. These come in different sizes and textures so we can practice our balance, as if we were on a tightrope. There are also real vines so that we can practice swinging from branch to branch, like trapeze artists. We can climb from hammock to hammock, stopping to rest when we need to. Just like in the wild, there are little "baskets" where several branches meet, and anteaters can make those places into napping nooks or branch baskets.

℅ **THE JUNGLE HOUSE:** This outdoor enclosure is the next best thing to the wild. There are tons of trees to climb, an amazing vine system, and all the plants and smells that we'll live with after release. When we get to the jungle house, we'll hardly ever see Ella anymore. If we're raised from babies, we must stay in this enclosure before we're released. Gabi was here, but I won't need to be; I'll just go straight back to the rainforest.

Once Ella had built all of these spaces for Gabi and perfected them, she realized that she'd built Tamandua Refuge, and she'd be ready for the next tamandua that came along.

TØ EACH HeR øwn

No matter which space we're living in, as individuals we do things a little differently. Here are a few of Gabi's quirks when she was living in the house (hey, no judgment).

- She created her own version of hide-and-seek. She'd sneak up and grab Ian's hand or arm, giving it a tug or a squeeze. She'd roll around; then she'd run away and hide just around the corner; then she'd start the

game again. (Maybe she liked this because we're such good hiders in the canopy.)

- She always tried to lick behind Ella's ear.

- She couldn't resist the taste of Ella's skin when Ella had salty sweat on it.

- When Ella gave her a tiny taste of olive oil or coconut oil, she would lick the outside of the container and Ella's hands, smacking her lips and frantically trying to get every drop.

But once Gabi made it to the jungle house, all of this stopped. By that point, there was no overlap between her world and the human world.

CHAPTER 5

PICKY EATERS' PICNIC

In the weeks after Gabi's rescue, the rainy season went on and on. Gabi seemed to hate climbing on rainy days; maybe it was because her claws slipped off the wood. So Ella had plenty of time in the kitchen to experiment with different combinations of food. It took her weeks to figure out what Gabi really should—and would—eat.

The formula of pups' diets has to be as close to our moms' milk as possible, with all the same vitamins, such as potassium, vitamin D, and vitamin K (found in termites!). To make sure that Gabi was getting everything she needed, Ella took her back

to the doctor for blood work. If a certain vitamin was low, Ella added more of it to Gabi's diet.

We anteaters have low metabolisms; this means that our bodies turn food into energy

It's fun to hack open a watermelon with your claws.

slowly. When we're adults, this helps us to be able to survive completely on insects. We get plenty of those in the wild, of course, but they don't have too many calories.

Gabi was fed a mixture of fruit juices, yogurt, and dog and cat foods, first separately and then in combinations. Ella experimented until she found a formula that was as close to a natural rainforest diet as she could get, though the "perfect" recipe is different for each of us.

Gabi ate her "mush mash" by flicking her tongue in and out of the container, as if it were a termite nest!

One thing hasn't changed from Gabi's days. If we anteaters had even one little tooth, it would be called a sweet tooth! We love fruit . . . and we hate all vegetables.

MUSH MASH

- 2 cups dried dog food
- ½ cup flax seed
- ¼ cup yogurt
- watermelon
- papaya juice
- banana
- water

Combine the first two ingredients, turning them into a powder. Mash in the yogurt, watermelon, papaya juice, banana, and water until it looks like baby food. Store in refrigerator in a sealed container.

Once a week, add tomato for acidity. When needed, blend in papaya seeds to prevent stomach parasites.

Most of all, we're just superpicky, so Ella has to keep daily records of what's working and what's not. When we're taken into captivity like this, many of us get weak and some of us die. It's almost as if our brains are attached to our termite nests in the wild.

Ella says she should just hang up a fancy menu.

The Rainforest Rescue Café

Mush Mash!

The Gabi Special Yogurt Mixed with Water

Sanctuary Smoothies

Whole, chopped, mashed, or combined for you in a smoothie any way you wish. Termites can be added to any smoothie.

- overripe avocado (*Gabi could smell one being cut in another room!*)

- coconut oil or coconut water (*perfect for sneaking in medicine*)

- soft, young coconuts already broken (*oily and mushy . . . mmm*)

- pitaya (*dragon fruit*)

- papaya

- overripe banana

- watermelon (*try it Gabi-style: mixed with lime juice.*)

- apple

- pineapple

- cucumber

- lime

- spinach (*great for vitamin K*)

- tomato

- cohune nuts with tiny termite-filled holes

- fermented orange (*This is a very special treat. It's just like what you might find on the rainforest floor. It's easier to open than a "fresh" orange, and you may get a gourmet surprise inside, such as ants or the larva of a wasp. Yum!*)

Please eat until your belly is full. I can tell you're done when your tummy is tight and round, like a ball!

You can get
lost in a
fermented
orange.

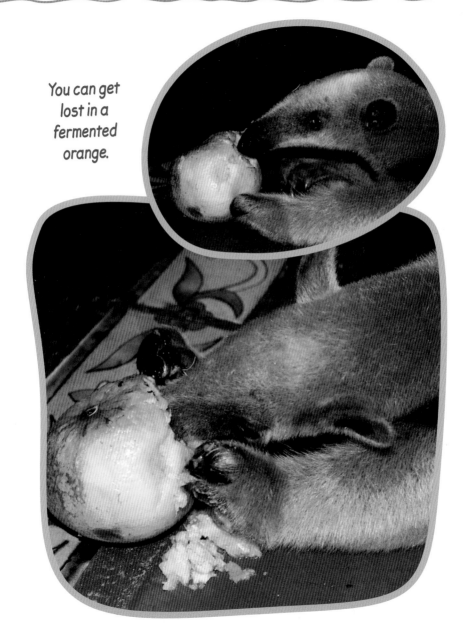

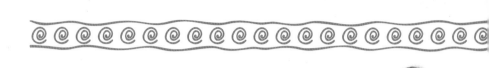

Wednesday

It poured all afternoon. I showed Gabi how to hack a watermelon open with her claws, and she loved it. She spent almost two hours straight mushing it and eating it. Then the same thing with the orange! She ate one whole orange and left the peel.

I also offered her one-quarter of a dragon fruit, but she ignored it.

She takes forty minutes to lick and mash her fruit, and forty more to clean between her claws and brush the rest of her fur, all with her tongue. She's as clean as a cat. She takes good care of her black clackers. She also holds her tail with her front claws and licks off sand and dirt.

PLAN: Continue introducing all fruits that she'd find in her natural habitat. Rotate her favorites. Most fruits seem mushy enough for her to eat, but she mushes them even more with her claws.

Fermented lime ... also divine.

Both Ella and Gabi took mealtime very seriously. This was good for me, because by the time I arrived, Ella was running a five-star rainforest restaurant ... for insectivores with no teeth.

CHAPTER 6

TERMITE TRAPPING

Of course, our *real* diet is all about termites and ants, so eventually we start eating them for a few hours every day. Here at the refuge, we get outstanding room service. And once in a while, if we eat a certain kind of ant or termite, we get so calm and relaxed that we go into a mysterious trance! Ella thinks there is a particular chemical that causes our bodies to react this way, but no one really knows for sure.

As I recovered, I felt like a queen. I ate all night long, on and off. Ella had *five* different termite nests for me to try, all in different parts of the room, so I had options, just

like in the wild. Plus, she had piles of ferns, heliconias, and rotten sticks, all crawling with even more termites. I'd just waddle from nest to nest all night, enjoying every flavor.

A termite nest is also a nice place to sip coconut water.

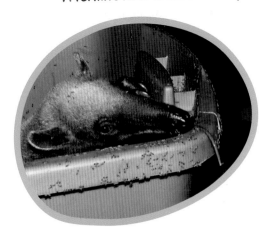

There is nothing about termite tubs that I don't like.

77

Sometimes, when I've already gobbled up all the termites in a nest,
I just make myself at home inside of it.

To the Anteaters, from Ella

Feeling Wild?

Insectivores' Specials

You're called an anteater, but here in Belize you eat more termites than anything else. The only ants here are tree ants, and you can get more food from termite mounds and nests. So I'll give you a termite taste test. You can let me know which you prefer, and I'll do my best to find them for you: flying ones, creamy white ones, light brown ones, ones that are hard inside, spongy ones, skinny ones, fat ones, small ones, big ones, and so on.

Unfortunately, not everything is available in all seasons, but I will try to deliver your favorites until you can get back out there to hunt them on your own.

Don't worry, fire ants are *never* on the menu. We know better than that.

Also available:

- honey
- a variety of juicy, protein-filled beetle larvae and grubs from rotten logs . . . anteater candy!

Bon appétit! When you're finished, I'll brush the extra termites off your fur just the way your mom would, so you won't get bit.

Room Service for Rescued Anteaters

By Ella

1. Set out a variety of nests and notice which the anteater eats from. Stick a few fingers right into that nest and let a few termites crawl onto you before you go out hunting for more. Roll some between your fingers and smell them so you remember what to look for. Don't freak out.

2. Put your termite tubs, garbage bags, machete, and water bottle into the truck and find Don Luis Hernandez, whom loves animals and knows the jungle. Together, drive about twenty minutes to the citrus fields. The drive is muddy and rocky—be prepared to get out a few times to push the truck.

3. Together, walk up and down the citrus grove looking for nests. Like an anteater, use the map in your head that tells you

Don Luis will do almost anything to get us our meals.

where they are. When you see one, go check what kind of termite it is (if you have a good mental map, this won't be necessary—you'll just know). Keep going till you find the right one.

4. One person hacks off a chunk of the nest while the other holds the garbage bag underneath to catch it. Place the chunk into the tub. Add the rotten branches they were eating from on the tree, plus some ferns for them to hide in. (If they're not happy, they'll try to climb out of the tub.) Put the bin in the back of the truck. Repeat until you have five nests.

5. Once home, make a moat so the termites can't crawl out and get all over your house. Put the tubs with the nests inside bigger tubs filled with water. (This does not always work—sometimes a small group of termites will form a little bridge and rescue others in their colony. The

bridge-builders die, but they've saved the others in their colony. Very kind.) Put the tubs in different areas of the pen.

6. Repeat every other day until the anteater is released.

The anteaters, of course, are the natural trappers. Carefully observe them using their gooey tongues to pull the insects up out of the nests! This never gets boring.

As I mentioned, I get excellent room service. But during my recovery from surgery, there

was only one problem. The termites were crawling onto my scars, which hadn't healed yet.

Ella finally bought me some baby pajamas. Her Facebook friends found this very entertaining, but to Ella, it was just a logical solution. I was still weak and couldn't use my leg to balance or climb onto the termite nest, so Ella supported my body with her hands and propped me up on the nest. I really took

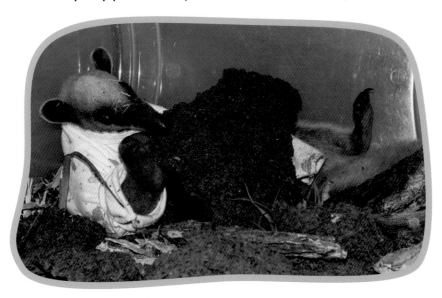

Pajama party—all termites invited!

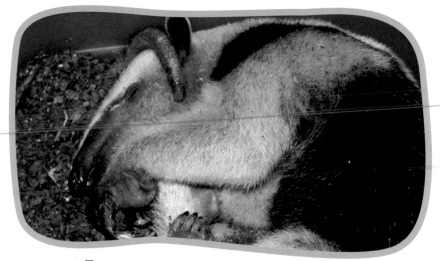

Termites can be tiring . . . but once our bellies are finally full, our tails make good pillows.

my time, too. Ella's legs would fall asleep.

As I healed, though, it was harder to stay calm. I moved into the little pen so I could finally start climbing a bit. A few weeks later, I moved to the big pen. I love climbing on the hammocks and all the dry lianas here. I love the dry log that I can squeeze and hack, making a *click, click, click* sound. It's great practice for what will come next.

PART 3

REHABILITATION

School Days

CHAPTER 7

FIELD TRIPS
TO THE FUTURE

Ella has great respect for our anteater pace. We can't be trained like dogs. Instead, it's the wild animals who train and teach the humans. Ella tells vet students that if they have the patience to watch and listen, they can learn everything they need to know about helping tamanduas.

Gabi had a lot to learn, so for a few months, Ella took her to the citrus fields almost every single day. (I was older, and my mom had already taught me to climb and dig for termites, so I haven't needed field trips like Gabi's.) After a while Gabi became more independent, spending more time away from Ella, but as soon as something went wrong, of course, she climbed straight onto Ella's head.

LESSON PLAN:
ANTEATER FIELD TRIPS

By Ella

For: Private Tutors of Rescued Anteaters

Time: up to four hours

What you'll need: patience and water

Take rescued anteaters on field trips so they can learn and practice wild behavior. Pick the same place to go every day, one that is similar to where you'll release the anteater eventually. On each trip, try to do as many of these activities as possible:

🐾 **Mental Maps:** Walk with anteaters so they can create their own mental maps of where the termite nests or ant mounds are. After just a few trips they'll find and recognize them. They'll sniff the nooks between cracks of rocks and wet wood, too, looking everywhere. They'll be very methodical about it—they have a plan.

🐾 **Hack & Crack:** Show the anteaters how to get food. Take their paws and show them

These claws are made for hacking.

how to use their claws like little axes to open the nests. You'll only have to show them once!

🐾 **Get a Grip & Hang in There:** The anteaters should be able to "wrap and hang" with their strong tails. (Tutor tip: Be the anteater! On one field trip I spent thirty minutes upside down, trying to see the world through Gabi's eyes.)

It's a process.

90

In the wild, if a predator gets too close, anteaters might hiss.

🐾 **De-fense! De-fense!:** Anteaters must learn to defend themselves. If they feel threatened, they'll stand straight up, arch their backs, and hold their arms out wide in order to look as big as possible. They might also wheeze or drool.

What goes up . . .   *. . . must come down.*

🐾 **Climbing & Balance:** As time goes on, you'll notice your anteater improve, making better choices about the "right" branches to hold on to.

🐾 **Snooze-fest:** Let them fall asleep in the branches, if they like. In the wild, when not foraging, anteaters also den in holes and hideaways in the hollow trees or the ground.

- 🐾 **Insect Identification:** Anteaters must learn to recognize different species of insects. (Little Gabi's fur didn't protect her against fire ants or big black ants, but eventually she learned to avoid those nests.)

- 🐾 **Other snacks:** The anteater might try other snacks besides termites and ants, such as cocoa pods or fermented fruit, another sign that he or she is preparing well for release.

Warning! As pups grow, they'll be less likely to cling to your head and neck and more likely to climb high and stay high. That's good, but you have to watch them very closely. It's easy to lose sight of them, and sometimes they manage to climb on trees that are too big for them. Then they can't climb down, so, obviously, you have to climb up to get them.

If I got to go on field trips, my favorite part would be the termites. Gabi got to have her own little treasure hunt every day! She also found food on termite highways, where the insects travel in lines right up and down trees. (When humans think of ants, they think of anthills on the ground, but arboreal ants live in trees, under moss. The ants in anthills are too aggressive for us. We also love the larvae of wasp nests, but we have to watch out for the wasps!)

YUMMY TUNNELS

Termite tunnels (or "mud tubes") are underground miniature cities made of hard soil. The termites work together to create this whole system, protecting themselves from predators. They have rooms and tunnels, and they can also go all the way up a tree. They're like a protective path connecting the nest with the food outside. Termite tunnels can be up to sixty feet (18 meters) long!

We love the insects, but we never totally destroy their nests. That would be silly, for if we did, where would our food be? So we eat just enough, and we let the colony regrow. In this way, we're like sustainability farmers—human farmers who grow and harvest crops without hurting the environment or destroying habitats.

Anyway, termite hunting isn't always a party in every bite. As soon as we start eating from a nest, there's the risk of the termites coming out to bite us as they protect their colony. When that happens, we have to run away and start on the next nest. Also, we might get a nasty surprise when we eat a foul-tasting insect (that taste is what protects them from us predators)!

Termite hunting isn't always fun and games for Ella, either. A few weeks ago, when she came home with my termites, she was in the worst mood.

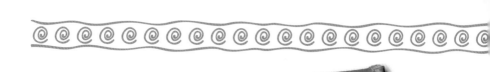

Monday Afternoon

Feeling angry at other humans. The citrus farmers have sprayed their crops with pesticides, killing all the termites in their nests. It took me three hot hours (in 99 percent humidity) to find a nest with live termites. When I finally found one and tried to hack some of it off, I stepped in fire ants and got horrible bites.

I finally got some pieces of nest, but it's frustrating. It's so hard to rehabilitate and release the tamanduas, and now their food is poisoned.

CHAPTER 8

JUNGLE GYMS

When Gabi wasn't on a field trip feasting on fresh termites, she was in her pen developing her balance and strength. It's like being in Anteater Circus School.

Gabi resting in the jungle house. See how our paw pads have folds down the center to help us grasp narrow branches and vines?

Gabi's high-wire act in the jungle house.

In the wild, our paws let us move quietly
across the canopy. We may move in slow
motion, but we're natural, graceful acrobats.

98

Sloths move this way too. We're like air ballerinas.

In the big pen, Gabi did well in Anteater Circus School and soon graduated to the jungle house, which Ella designed herself. It's as much like the wild as possible. Ella began to sense that Gabi was just putting up with her, no longer really *wanting* to be with her. Gabi was climbing on Ella less and barely wanted to play anymore. She was hearing the call of the wild.

In the jungle house, there are more hiding places than in the pens. It's built around three trees, and Ella planted even more things: bananas, heliconias (which ants love), and hibiscus. Hibiscus branches grow fast, so it's okay if we break them. She also cemented in some old orange trees for termite breeding grounds.

99

The top three reasons Gabi loved the jungle house?

- **Lianas!** Lianas are thick, ropy vines that grow up, around, and between trees, looping around their trunks and branches. We wrap our tails around them tight and swing from tree to tree. In the indoor pens, the branches were close to the ground and the termite box stayed on the floor. Gabi could eat safely without having to work too hard to balance. But here, she could do everything up high, climbing so much higher than in the pens, so she could practice protecting herself in the actual canopy.

- **Nice And Dry!** She never got wet. The jungle house is covered in a tarp, just like the canopy. And flaps protected her from strong wind.

- **Fermented Oranges!** When oranges drop from the tree, they ferment on the ground, where Gabi could hack them open and gobble them up. Plus, there's plenty of rotting wood—home for termites!—on the ground. The termites dig tunnels in wet cohune logs. Gabi would crack at the wood and find beetles, larvae, and ants.

Gabi spent lots of time in this log ... butt out!

But one thing that *no* anteater would like about the jungle house is the ceiling, which is very firmly attached. A few, including Gabi, have tried to push it up and off, and a few times they've broken some of the metal staples. It's a hint to Ella that the wildness is just bursting out of them!

But no matter which area we're living in, Ella keeps most humans away from us and keeps watching us to see how well we climb, balance, eat, and sleep up high. If we're not excelling at all of those things, we can't go back out there just yet.

Gabi excelled in the jungle house, and after just a few months she was released for good.

PART 4

RELEASE

Graduation

CHAPTER 9

DRIVE TO THE WILD
Two Weeks Later

And, apparently, I've been excelling, too! For the last week, Ella's been obsessed with choosing exactly the right place to release me.

Before the hurricane, she had a spot all picked out, and then everything changed because of the floods. But as always, she has a plan B. A few days ago, she, Don Luis, and Marvin drove thirty minutes and hiked two hours to check out another spot deep in the mountains. It's far from roads and people. It's also not far from where Gabi was released.

They made sure that the trails were clear for them, and they used their machetes to hack away plants and branches so they

*Ella and her staff picked what they thought
would be the perfect spot.*

wouldn't fall or get stuck when they carried
me along the path. If we bounce and jostle
too much in our carriers on the hike, we'll flip
out. And we have to be in a relaxed state of
mind when we're released.

At night, Ella feeds me a ton of termites,
way more than usual. It will be my final feast

inside the pen. I hear her get up ten times in the night and tell Ian that she's nervous, but she knows I'm ready.

At sunrise, she shuffles into the kitchen and cuts an avocado in quarters. Ian follows her and starts the coffee, and Ella's so anxious that he makes her stop and give him a long hug. She puts one-quarter of the avocado into my pen. She spreads another quarter on toast and tries to eat it herself, but she takes only a few bites.

Ella opens my travel carrier and puts two T-shirts from the pen and the other two quarters of avocado inside. I go right in, really just for the avocado. But before I know it, she

closes the wire door behind me and covers
the whole thing in an old blanket. I can't see a
thing outside this little cage.

But I do see the tiny hole I hacked in the
carrier on the way to my second surgery! I
see that Ella's covered it with duct tape, but
that's unimportant. I'll chip away at this hole
as long as I'm kept here. I'll just focus on that.

Now I'm being picked up and carried. I'm
swaying back and forth more than I'd prefer,
but Ella's being careful, especially on the wet
stairs. Don Luis and Marvin are waiting at the
truck, which is already running and ready to
go. But Ella's still preoccupied.

"There must be something I'm forgetting," she
says to Marvin.

"Come on, Ella!" he says, laughing. Apparently

she's been like this with every anteater
since Gabi.

She sits next to me in the back seat while
Don Luis drives. We're talking without words
again. She holds her hand near the crate so
I can smell her, and I relax a little. But I'm still
so excited that I keep poking my legs out the
wire door of the crate and slowly working
on my hole. I'm making progress. The guys
in the front seat are laughing about this, but
Ella doesn't even hear them. Right now, she's
dead serious.

CHAPTER 10

THE SLOW SHUFFLE

Once we park, the guys stick a long pole through the top of the carrier so they can carry me on the two-hour hike. Ella goes first, to make sure the path isn't too slippery. "It's not so bad," she calls back to them. "But remember to keep the carrier up high so you won't drop it if you slip. If you do slip, make sure you fall the right way! You can't jostle her! She'll be very upset!"

"Gee, thanks for thinking of us, Ella." Marvin laughs, but Ella doesn't seem to notice the joke.

"What's she doing?" she calls. "Is she still hacking away at that hole?"

"You bet," Marvin answered. "I just peeked. It's like the size of my thumbnail!"

The humans move slowly and carefully. I work on my hole with my right leg and keep poking my left leg through the wire door. My claws tap and clack against the metal bars. The smell of the humans' sweat is strong. Eventually I get tired from all my hacking, and I start to snooze. When I wake up, my carrier's on solid ground, but it's still covered in the blanket. The humans are whispering.

"Now you have to get into her universe, her zone," Ella tells the others. Her voice is quiet but intense. "We have to be anteaters and consider the place from her perspective. We'll look for the nests now. Then we pick exactly where to open the carrier."

More whispers.

"Stay quiet when you find termites," Ella

The hike goes on and on . . . and on.

warns. "Just point and wiggle your hands like little bugs; that's the signal."

It takes them a while to find a tree with my favorite termites. When they finally do, they move the carrier to the base of the tree, and Ella pulls back the blanket a little. She opens the gate quickly, pops in a tiny chunk of termite nest, closes the gate, and watches me. I sniff the nest, but I'm too distracted to eat.

Because now I know it for sure. It's all finally happening. I can't believe I made it back.

Marvin and Don Luis walk about thirty steps away from Ella. She stays sitting next to me; then she moves the cover away bit by bit. The rainforest air and light slowly pour into my dark little cage. We sit this way for about thirty minutes. The three humans have arranged themselves in a triangle position

Gabi's carrier, moments before they opened the door.

so that they have the best chance of keeping their eyes on me once I go up. They have their binoculars and cameras ready; they're each trying to get a good view. After releasing thirteen other anteaters, Ella's perfected this whole process, and she teaches her helpers what to do.

Marvin's and Don Luis's footsteps crunching the leaves on the rainforest floor may be the last human sounds I'll ever hear. Ella slowly opens the wire door, and I inch toward her hand, forward, out of the cage, toward my real home.

I'm already forgetting about the inside of this carrier. No more plastic for me! Even the hole I've worked so hard on is a distant memory.

Just as Gabi did ten years ago, I sniff Ella's hand. It's my last whiff of a human. Now all I want to do is breathe the fresh air in deep.

I smell ferns and rotten wood, hibiscus and jasmine.

I smell freedom.

CHAPTER 11
THE GREAT CANOPY CLIMB

Thirty seconds after that door opens, I'm headed *up up up*. The ground, a maze of roots covered in a blanket of leaves, branches, and twigs, is already below me. Everything makes perfect sense.

Like Gabi and most of the others, I don't pick the tree the humans thought I would. They don't know everything!

See, I'm already ten feet up, and oh gee, here's a big chunk of moss that I can stick my nose right into. Yes—juicy ants. Things are going great. I have a quick snack—I haven't had ants in so long. Ella couldn't deliver them to my pen the way she could with the termites. They're scrumptious.

Soon I'm twenty feet up, and I know exactly what to do. Every cell in my body hums with confidence. I keep going up, sniffing as fast and hard as I can with every inch. I smell everything all at once. I smell other creatures: ants, termites, howler monkeys, frogs, katydids, lizards, hummingbirds, kinkajous, and armadillos. I smell butterflies sipping nectar—their favorite party drink.

I smell the epiphytes I've missed so much. They all grow together on the same tree: orchids, bromeliads, lichens, moss, and ferns.

A wobbly branch is no reason to freak out. My tail balances me.
My paw pads perfectly grasp the branches and vines.
My leg feels just fine.

They cover the trunks and branches so much
you can barely see the bark—sometimes the
trees get so heavy with them that when it
rains, whole branches come down. They're
all glomming onto the trunks, reaching for the
light.

All these smells come together as they reach
my excellent, excellent nose. If humans could

117

I hit a few dead ends, but I'm okay.

figure out how to make a perfume that
smelled like this place, I bet they could sell a
single bottle for a million dollars.

I really want to keep climbing, but *oh no!* The
top of this tree must have snapped off in
the hurricane. I think I hear Ella's heart skip
a beat! But it's no problem. I just swing on
a liana over to the next one, using my best
circus moves. It's a minor detour up to the

canopy. This happens two more times until I finally make it to a tree that hasn't lost its top.

Whee! Here's a nap nook. The sun already feels so good on my fur. It's been such a long time. I'd love to bask in the sun, belly up in this branch basket, but I want to keep moving for a while. It's been so long since I've really moved!

Whee! Here's a good termite nest. I'll remember all this for later.

I'm having my own private canopy celebration. I dance among the lianas that grow toward the sun. I feast on more ants and offer a toast to the termites in their nests. The humid air hugs my whole body hard, and I groove to the music of the scarlet macaws. I cheer for the crickets and the cicadas. The ferns are my party decorations, as pretty and perfect as lace shawls.

Soon enough it will be dark, and this party will get even better. I remember night in the rainforest. The air cools, and it never gets totally dark. There's the moonglow and there are insects that light up like fireflies. There are even fungi that glow.

But that's hours from now. I'm in the moment, and all of a sudden I can climb no higher. But this time it's not because I've chosen a broken tree. I can't climb any higher because I'm on *top of the world!* I've poked my head right through the roof of the canopy. It feels as if the sun is giving me a big kiss, and the green surface looks like an ocean in front of me.

The sky stretches in all directions. I perch upon my giant emerald throne with perfect balance.

CHAPTER 12

UP, UP, AND AWAY

Monday, 4:30 p.m.

Marvin and Don Luis and I are still here, but Abi's gone. She's so high up in the canopy, we can't see her! For a few minutes one of us had her in sight and pointed to show the others where she was, but that ended fast.

We are so totally down here, and she is so totally up there. I bet she's above the canopy by now. It's their world up there, not ours.

I've been lying on the damp ground on my back, looking up, but I see only dusty rays of light coming

through the canopy. Whenever any light reaches the floor, plants at the bottom jump at the chance to grow. It's like a race for the light. Life seems to want to head up, up, up . . . just like the anteaters.

It's been an hour since she climbed to the canopy. When we followed her and she heard our footsteps, she froze. That's not normal; she should always be on the move. So we stopped following her.

We brought some granola bars, but until now we were too focused on the release to remember to eat, plus we had to be quiet with the wrappers. Now we're hungry. We unwrap them and crunch away!

Every release is different, but they're all the same too. You want to stay forever. When we released Gabi, we packed to stay overnight, and we stayed for ten hours watching for any sign of her! We want to protect them, but the whole point is that they don't need us anymore.

With every release, I feel as if the jungle air immediately erases the tamandua's memories of the human world. Then I go home to the empty pen.

This release went quite smoothly. But I miss Abi. I

knew her so well. For months, I tried to live in her brain.

There will be more storms and more human danger. And there will always be natural predators such as eagles, hawks, and boas. But storms and predators are part of normal life in the wild, and that's the only life an anteater should have. I don't want any more of them to be hurt, but I know they probably will be. So I hope I get to help one hundred more the way I helped the first fourteen.

Like Abi, Gabi went up fast. Maybe they'll meet up there someday.

THE NEXT DAY

TO: Abe Friesen

FROM: Ella Baron

Dear Mr. Abe,

I hope you and your family and your property are all safe after the hurricane. We humans are all fine, but we had plenty of injured wildlife to help, plus lots of damage to our property.

I wanted to share some good news, though. The tamandua you saved ten weeks ago finally got her freedom yesterday when we brought her back to the wild.

Her leg had been broken, and she needed two surgeries. The rehabilitation process was not always easy, but none of it would have happened if you hadn't made that first phone call. You saved this little tamandua from certain death, and then I did my part by getting her to the docs and rehabilitating her.

We released her in an area far from humans and roads, and she was very confident in her climbing. You wouldn't even recognize her. She is superstrong and very large (eight pounds). You'd never know that she'd once had a broken leg and an injured eye.

We zoomed in with our cameras—she was already twenty or thirty feet above the ground when we photographed her. As you know, if a tamandua stays low to the ground, something's wrong.

Once again, thank you for your help. By the way, we named her Abi . . . after you.

Gratefully,

Ella Baron

A LETTER FROM THE AUTHOR.
HUMANS PLAN, NATURE LAUGHS

Most visitors to Belize never get to see an anteater unless they go to the Belize Zoo.

When I traveled to Belmopan to meet Ella and Abi, I planned to observe the anteater constantly. I planned to observe Ella's every move. I planned to interview others involved in wildlife rescue and learn everything I could about the ecosystem and habitat of the rainforest. It was a research trip, and I brought several notebooks and extra pencils. I made sure I had lots of space on my phone for new photos and video of every little thing.

I planned, I planned, I planned . . . and in the end I learned that humans can't really plan anything.

Three days after I arrived, a category 1 hurricane named Hurricane Earl devastated Caves Branch, taking all night long to do its full damage. The staff evacuated the guests at the lodge. I had already decided to stay for the rest of my planned trip— another five days—to try to help in the recovery effort.

The storm began late at night, and Ella told me to try to get some sleep. As the sun rose, she woke me with the bad news. Most of the surrounding canopy had come down, and the damage to the property seemed very bad. As the bad news kept coming in, I sat on the living room floor near Abi's pen and watched her wake up. I knew that Abi should be the one to tell this story.

These were horrible, exhausting, muddy days for Ella and Ian and their staff. Luckily, no humans at Caves Branch were hurt, but the property—which is how Ella and Ian make their living—was seriously damaged. Her precious botanical gardens were almost completely destroyed. We spent days trying to rescue birds, opossum, and snakes. Sometimes we could get the animals fixed up and back out there, but there were too many times when we couldn't. At the end of each day, I cried in my cold shower. Then I'd go to bed early so I could try to be of some help the next day.

During the worst moments of that week, Ella never stopped being a teacher. She gave me a crash course in wildlife rescue and disaster recovery, and she led her entire staff—almost one hundred people, if you counted the men from neighboring villages who came with their chainsaws to clear away the fallen trees.

And whenever she had a minute, Ella told me more of Gabi's story. I knew I wanted to write about her, because now I knew what a flood (and a rainforest hurricane!) looked, sounded, and felt like.

The trip wasn't what I'd planned, but I learned much more than I'd expected to. I think that the more you learn and the more you teach, the more you can do for our environment—and every creature in it.

And I hope everyone who reads this book someday gets to observe and learn amazing things from unusual animals (including humans) . . . just, with any luck, not in a hurricane!

— Kama Ainhum

Hurricane recovery, Day 3.
Me, Ella, and her machete.

THREE QUICK QUESTIONS FOR ELLA BARON

Q: If tamanduas could talk, what do you think would be the most important thing they could tell humans?

A: *We would never come to hurt you, so don't hurt us! When you cut down the rainforest, you destroy our homes and our food supply. Then we have no place to go, and we end up in your yards, where the dogs attack us, or we have to cross the highways, where we get hit by cars.*

Q: What do you say to people who think having a tamandua refuge in your home is odd?

A: *I explain it this way: human kids love to play outside, but when they're sick, they have to stay home and let their parents take care of them. The same with tamanduas. While they are recovering, I take care of them twenty-four hours a day, protecting them from being wet or too hot or too cold and from insects and snakes. What better place for them than home?*

Q: Running a sanctuary is tough. Is it worth it?

A: *As there are still humans who hurt tamanduas, somebody has to protect them. Why not me? Yes, it's a very tough job. But I think each of us must try to do something to protect wildlife, so I am just doing my part.*

128

HOW YOU CAN HELP

- Learn more at tamanduarefuge.org and tamanduaworldatcavesbranch.blogspot.com/.

- **Zoos are not the only way to learn about wildlife!** You may not live near an anteater sanctuary, but there are animal sanctuaries everywhere. Learn about the animals that share your habitat, and find shelters and sanctuaries near you that help them. Also, tell others that wild animals are not pets.

- **Every year, Belize loses almost fifty square miles of rainforest habitat, and it's getting worse annually.** If your family is buying furniture, decks, or floors, suggest that they check the type of wood they are made from. If it's rainforest tropical hardwood (such as mahogany or teak), consider an alternative.

- **If your family's planning a trip to Central or South America (or anywhere!) and you want to see native animals, make sure you visit only places where animals live natural lives.** Research the places you hear and read about, and write to them and ask questions. Some places call themselves sanctuaries, but they actually keep healthy animals in captivity in order to make money (by doing such things as

letting tourists take selfies with the animals). With a grownup, search online (search "responsible tourism" or "sustainable tourism" plus the name of the country).

- **When you're observing any animal in its habitat, no matter how friendly the animal may seem,** lower your voice, move slowly, don't feed it, and take your trash with you.

- **Choose projects and reports about the rainforest so you can learn more and teach others.** Visit a botanical garden that has rainforest plants. (Rainforests cover 6 percent of the earth's surface but are home to half of the plant and animal species on Earth.)

- **Reduce, reuse, recycle.** Waste affects the environment and every creature in it in many ways. There are 7.5 billion people on our planet . . . that's a lot of trash, and we're running out of room for it all. Cutting back on the amount of garbage, finding new ways to use it, and recycling helps all living things.

HOW TO DRAW AN ANTEATER

1. Draw an eggplant shape for the body.

2. Add two smaller eggplant shapes for legs.

3. Erase the two leg marks and add a curved line for the tail.

4. Finish the tail.

5. Add two lines to show the anteater's markings, and draw the front claw. Erase the back leg mark.

6. Draw the rest of the claws and the face.

GLOSSARY

biodiversity: the variety of life in a habitat or ecosystem.

bromeliad: the most common epiphytes (see definition below).

canopy: the "ceiling and roof" of the rainforest, which is formed by a thick layer of treetops.

captivity: being kept by humans (as in zoos or as pets); the opposite of living in the wild.

climate: the weather pattern over a long period of time.

conservation: preserving, protecting, or restoring.

deforestation: cutting down forests so that humans can use the land or the wood from trees.

ecosystem: a community of animals and plants that live together in an area; a system in which living things interact with the weather, the sun, the air, the water, and the soil around them.

environment: the surroundings in which people or animals live.

epiphyte: plants that grow on tree branches high up in the canopy. Epiphytes don't grow from soil; they get water and nutrients from the sun and the moisture in the air.

habitat: the natural home of an animal.

humidity: the amount of moisture (water vapor) in the air.

insectivore: an animal that eats insects.

liana: a strong, thick climbing vine that grows on and between trees, up toward the sun.

metabolism: the way a body digests food and uses it for energy.

nocturnal: sleeping during the day and being awake at night.

predator: an animal that eats other animals.

prehensile: able to wrap and cling, like an anteater's tail.

protect: keep from harm.

recover: get better.

refuge: a safe place.

rehabilitate: return to one's natural condition.

release: let go.

rescue: save or help.

sanctuary: a safe place.

subsistence farming: growing just enough food for one's own needs.

tendril: a coiled shoot from a climbing plant that lets it cling to another plant and climb toward the light.

treatment: the way a person behaves toward others.

welfare: the health and happiness of a living thing.

TRY SOME KRIOL

Most Belizeans speak and understand the Kriol ("CREE-ole") language. Once a British colony, Belize gained independence in 1981. Even though English is the official language, Kriol brings together all of Belize's different ethnic groups. The Kriol language came from the Kriol people, who are a mix of the British colonial slaveholders and African slaves. The Africans lived close to their British slaveholders, and they began speaking their own version of English—a mix of what the British spoke and their own African dialect. Here's what Kriol looks and sounds like:

Gud maanin: Good morning.

Weh di gaan an?: What's up?

Aarite: All right.

Evryting gud/Evryting aarite: Everything's fine.

Chol! What on earth!

Da weh time?: What time is it?

Mi naym da . . . : My name is . . .

Si yoo lata: See you later.

Weh . . . : Where is . . .

Fu Chroo?: Really? Is that right?

Weh gaan ahn? or Weh di go ahn?: Hello/What's up?

Wahnti wahnti kyah geti an geti geti nuh wahnti: You always want what you can't have.

Sleep wit' yo' own eye: Only rely on what you know, not what others tell you.

One one craboo fill barrel: Every little bit counts [craboo is a Belizean fruit].

Betta no litta: Don't litter.

BiBLi00RAPHY

Brockmann-Fairchild, Jane. *All About Anteaters.* Rainbow Library. CreateSpace Independent Publishing Platform, 2017.

Greenwood, Elinor. *Eye Wonder: Rainforest.* New York: DK Publishing, 2013.

Gregory, Josh. *Anteaters.* Children's Press Paperback, 2014.

McIntyre, Gina. *The Anteater Fact & Picture Book: Fun Facts for Kids About Anteaters.* Turn and Learn, 2017.

PHOTO CREDITS

ACKNOWLEDGMENTS

Special thanks to:

Ella and Ian, who said yes

Enrique Acevedo

David Amaya

Robert Bacchas

Gabe Baron, whose bedroom I moved into during the flood

Abe Friesen

Pascual Garcia

Don Luis Hernandez

Junior Lopez

Dr. Julio Mercado, DVM

Dr. Maritza Navarro, DVM

Dr. Isabelle Paquet-Durand, DVM, Belize Wildlife &
Referral Clinic

Marvin Paredes

Tony & Therese Rath

Porfirio Reyes

Freddie Sanchez

Nikki Taieb and Sarah Kaye of the Staten Island Zoo

Lisa Williams

Dr. Philip DeSheild, DVM, and Dr. Jane Crawford, DVM,
Animal Medical Center

INDEX

⊚ TRUE TALES of RESCUE ⊚

Available now!

Coming soon!

photo credit: Nicholas Noyes

Kama Einhorn is a humane educator, animal welfare advocate, and author of more than forty books for children and teachers. Animals are her people. She lives in Brooklyn, New York.